SCIWORDS

THE 40+Topics science Crosswords

Bishnu Goswami

SCIWORDS

THE 40+Topics science Crosswords

Bishnu Goswami

This page intentionally left blank

PREFACE

It fetches me a lot of pleasure to write this book on Sciwords, the crosswords for science. In this current age, science and technology is at the forefronts of the advances of humanity. The world is illuminated by the pregnant idea-seeds coming from researchers, startups and applied-science companies. It is therefore very apt to be in the know about what science has to offer as a whole, even if we don't know all of the stuff in all of the details.

With the gradual decline in traditional outputs of information, in the form of newspapers and magazines, kids and youngsters these days have narrowed down on the internet for getting all their out-of-curriculum knowledge. The Internet is a vast ocean of information, and the traditional outputs are minuscule in comparison. However, it is important to note that we lose a quality battle in many cases in this process of transition. Unless we are actively promoting the study of scientific concepts, terms and techniques from the right places, either for ourselves or when we let young learners learn, we might be faltering, at least to some extent.

In this book, there is the compilation of crosswords from more than forty different topics of science. The level of the puzzles is not for the very beginners, although many are marked as school-level so that it becomes more accessible for students in middle or high school. As the topics do require a basic understanding of the subjects, the crosswords have not been made too complex to balance the difficulty.

Have a great time solving or let your near and dear ones test their acumen against Sciwords!

INTRODUCTION

Sciwords, a portmanteau of the words science and crosswords , is for people who are interested in knowing science and have a passion to solve puzzles. This can be you, your family, friends or the youngsters who live in a world of constant curiosity. Spanning over 40 different science topics, from Agricultural Science, to Economics, Particle Physics and Zoology, this book has the crosswords for almost all the broad subjects you are likely to come across in science. Let's start!

CONTENTS

Human Body
Internet
Inventors
Laboratory Science
Logic and Sets
Logic and Sets
Metals(School-Level)
Mobile Phones
Mobile Phones
Nursing
Particle Physics
Periodic Table
Physics
Physics
Planet Earth
Planet Earth
Programming
Psychology
SI units
Stars
Statistics
Statistics
Theory of Relativity
Windows
Windows
Zoology

ANSWERS

THE MAIN BOOK

Agricultural science

Agricultural science

ACROSS

3 A popular vehicle used to till the soil.
6 A type of machine used to harvest grains. It is also called a ___-harvester.
9 Organic matte created from the decomposition of corn husks, leaves etc.
10 This is the loss of fertilizers from the soil due to heavy rains and dilution.
11 A substance used to kill pests in agriculture.
12 A type of pest control which involves living organisms and low pollution risks.

DOWN

1 It is the research and development related to studying and improving plant-based crops.
2 A substance used to kill herbs and weeds in agriculture.
4 ___- farming involves planting at angles to the natural slope to cut soil erosion.
5 He is the father of Green revolution.
7 Plants such as beans and peas which can also fix nitrogen from the soil.
8 This is to be practiced in crop planting to keep the fertility of the soil. This involve
   cropping different crops in each round.

Animal Classification :Chordates

Animal Classification(Chordates)

ACROSS
4   One of the four chambers of a cow stomach.
7   A type of legless reptile which is known for its venom.
9   The turtle genus.
10 The genus of the cheetah.
11 A group of amphibians typically characterized by a lizard-like appearance.

DOWN
1   The subphylum for the animals with a backbone.
2   The largest order in Mammalia.
3   The class of animals which has feathers.
5   The property of milk production in mammals.
6   The genus of dogs.
7   The species name of humans.
8   Jawless vertebrates belong to this group.

Animal Classification: Nonchordates

Animal Classification(Nonchordates)

ACROSS

2 A protozoa which causes dysentery.
4 The repetition of internal body parts.
7 The phylum which hosts multi-cellular but usually asymmetrical organisms.
8 The scientific genus of honeybee.
9 The group of single -celled eukaryotic organisms.
10 The most basic taxonomic category.
11 The disease caused by the Plasmodium parasite, killing over a million every year
   worldwide.
12 The worm that causes disease for the eating of measly pork.

DOWN

1 The excretory organ in Annelids.
3 The largest phylum in terms of number of species.
5 The phylum where snails and slugs lie in.
6 The kingdom of prokaryotes.

Animals

Animals

ACROSS

3 The number of teeth of a mature horse.
4 This is a popular endangered animal from China.
7 A group of lions is called this.
8 A female fox is also termed this.
9 The first animal in orbit around the Earth.
10 During winter, many bears stay in this dormant state for months.

DOWN

1 The tongue of this animal is as big as an elephant!
2 This animal means "person of the forest".
3 This bird has the longest tongue and stays on one leg when resting.
5 A group of crows is called by this term.
6 This animal's scientific name means "sea-dog"
7 A group of wolves is called by this name.

Astronomy

Astronomy

ACROSS
3   This moon of Jupiter is found to contain an underground ocean.
7   Light-____ can greatly reduce the visibility of the night sky.
8   A star cannot have elements heavier than this in its core by simple nuclear fusion.
9   This is the largest galaxy in our local group which is set on a collision course with our own galaxy.
10 The top side when we look at the sky is called the ____.
11 This is the smallest planet of the solar system.
12 this is the largest moon in the solar system.

DOWN
1   This type of telescope, as opposed to reflecting ones, is often found in cheaper telescopes.
2   The bottom side when we look at the sky, facing the Earth is called the ____.
4   This is a very bright type of star where heavy elements such as Gold forms.
5   This is a part of the electromagnetic spectrum where heat is detected.
6   One of the fundamental forces, best explained by Einstein's theory of general relativity.

Biogeochemical Cycle
(School-Level)

Biogeochemical Cycle (School-Level)

ACROSS
5 Ocean waters ___, increasing the humidity level in the atmosphere.
7 Carnivores consume ___, which eats the plants.
10 In Ammonification, the ___-ion is produced, as a part of the nitrogen cycle.
11 The ___-cycle involves the yellowish element of the same name.
12 The ___-cycle involves respiration in living organisms.

DOWN
1 ___-bacteria convert complex compounds into simpler ones in the soil.
2 ___-Nitrogen in the air cannot betaken directly by plants.
3 The water-___ is the upper surface of the rocks underground over which water stays.
4 In the atmosphere , Nitrogen is converted into its ions by ___ strikes.
6 It is the total quantity or weight of organisms in a given area or volume.
8 The ___ cycle is an important biogeochemcial cycle in which photosynthesis reduces the amount in the atmosphere.
9 Aggregate of condensed water vapor that stores water in the atmosphere.

Biology

Biology

ACROSS
1 This system protects our body from diseases internally.
5 These organelles are called the powerhouse of the cell.
8 These type of cells cause a disease which is characterized by uncontrolled cell division.
10 It is a branch of biology which studies animals.
11 These are the unit of inheritance.

DOWN
2 Some cellular organelles can only be seen by this type of microscope.
3 This is a branch of biology which studies Fungi.
4 Chromosomes consists of these proteins and DNA.
5 The source of variation in a population.
6 Life originated about 4-__ years ago in Earth.
7 Organisms that form the bridge between living and non-living.
9 The leguminous plant over which Mendel did his famous experiments.

Cell(Biology)

Cell(Biology)

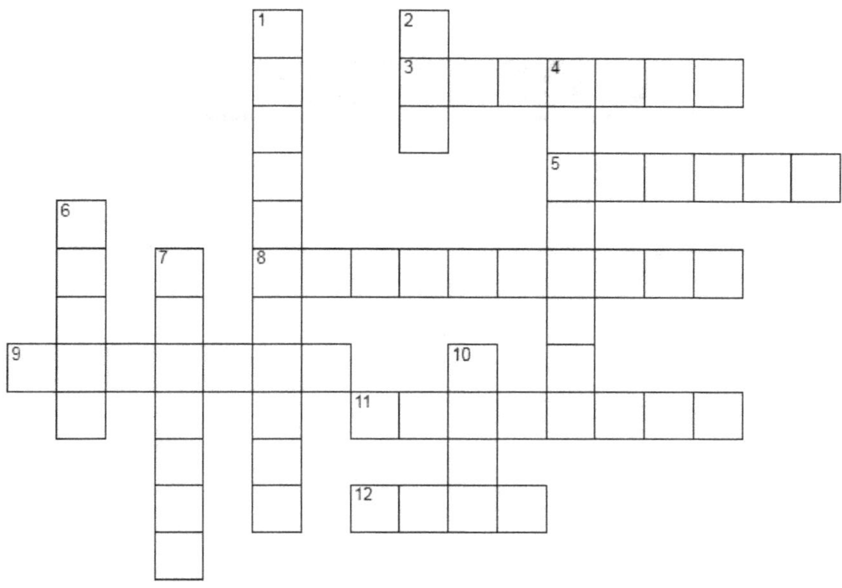

ACROSS
3   Referred to as the brain of the cell.
5   The storage polysaccharide in plants.
8   Humans have 23 pairs of these.
9   A type of cellular division which keeps the number of chromosomes the same.
11 A bunch of organelles for cellular mobility in bacteria, like a long hair.
12 Robert hook coined this term which means "small room".

DOWN
1   Genes are ___ into RNA.
2   The main nucleic acid for humans.
4   Called the suicide bags of cell.
6   The bilayer in cell membrane is chiefly made up of ___.
7   Ribosomes have this main function of synthesis of __.
10 The cell-___ is a strong outer layer of cells which is only present in plants.

Chemistry

Chemistry

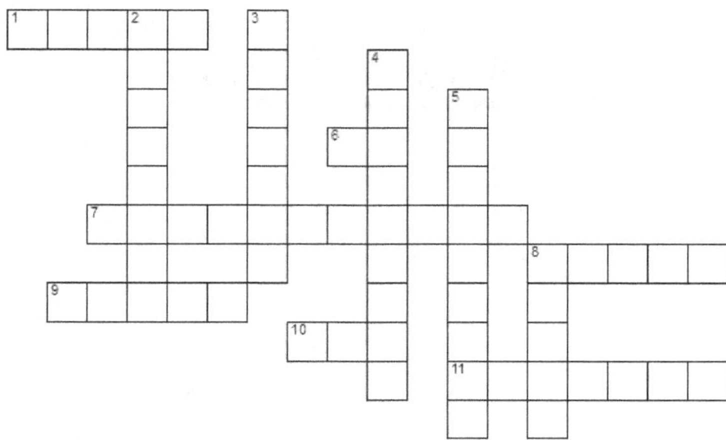

ACROSS

1 The ball and ___ model is widely used to visualize compounds.
6 The two letter which symbolizes Iron.
7 This is the process of transition of a substance directly from the solid to gas phase.
8 The law that states the amount of dissolved gas is proportional to its partial pressure is called ___'s law.
9 This is the radioactive noble gas.
10 It is a charges species which has gained or lost one or more electron(s).
11 It is a pure substance made up of only one kind of atoms.

DOWN

2 It is a pure substance made up of more than one kind of atoms.
3 Study of compounds based on a carbon skeleton is known as ___ chemistry.
4 Chemical reactions involve the exchange and sharing of ___.
5 He is known as the discoverer of Oxygen, and also is known as the father of modern chemistry.
8 A common process of production of ammonia using an iron catalyst in industries is called the ___'s process.

Clouds

Clouds

ACROSS

2 Cyclones have a central region of low ___.
5 This cloud in Latin means "a curl of hair".
7 The quintessential rain clouds.
8 This is the state which clouds remain, where droplets are suspended in a gas.
9 When clouds shine in multiple colors, like a soap bubble ,it is called cloud ___.
12 Most clouds remain in this layer of the atmosphere.

DOWN

1 These are also called thunderstorm clouds.
3 This low level, flat clouds looks like elevated fog.
4 The type of cloud that we use as the general symbol of clouds.
6 These are used to study clouds from above.
10 This is the center of a hurricane.
11 When low clouds touch the ground, they are called ___.

Cognitive Science

Cognitive Science

ACROSS
1 Space between two neurons where propagation occur by neurotransmitters.
3 This emotion involves feeling of compassion.
7 This emotion often results after a fight-or-flight response.
8 This is the scientific study of languages.
10 Part of brain involved in emotions such as fear.
11 This, in our brain, allows us to store information for later use.
12 This emotion lets us to get hot-headed.

DOWN
2 An integral part of cognitive science, involves the study of human mind and functions.
4 Artificial __ involves the study of cognition in machines.
5 An optical __ tricks our brain in what we see.
6 Douglas ___ wrote the famous book Godel, Escher, Bach.
9 It is a variety of language that is characteristic of a particular sample among the language speakers.

Computer hardware (school level)

Computer hardware(School Level)

ACROSS
3   The unit where the output is displayed in a computer.
7   This is a term used by hardware enthusiasts to increase the clock speed of a computer's processor or GPU.
8   A type of printer which uses Light Amplification by the Stimulated Emission of Radiation(Caps on purpose).
9   The acronym for a type of storage drive which is much faster than spin-based hard disks.
10 The type of lock in keyboard which is neither The Num lock nor the Caps lock.
11 An obsolete technology which the "A" drive usually pointed to.

DOWN
1   This is a computer peripheral that cools the components using a burst of air.
2   The P in CPU. It usually performs the most calculative operations in a computer.
4   A type of printer which uses jets of inks to print in paper.
5   An input device which is also the name of a biology lab animal model.
6   The U in USB stands for this.
8   A type of display technology which superseded CRT and made monitors much thinner than before.

Diet

Diet

ACROSS
2 Pescetarian dieters eat this cold-blooded animal.
4 The type of food that tastes good but is bad for health in large quantities.
6 Bears have this food habit as they eat both meat, fruits and other plant products.
9 This class of required food (in low doses) originate in the earth and cannot be made by living organisms.
11 For proper bowel movement, this item must be in enough quantities in the diet.

DOWN
1 Sugar is broken down to this simple carbohydrate in the body.
2 This is the common carbohydrate present in fruits.
3 The storage polymer which is made from carbohydrate in an animal body.
5 This short form represents the resting energy expenditure per unit time.
7 This is an essential component of diet in minute amounts and variants are represented by single letters.
8 The storage polymer which is made from carbohydrate in an plant.
10 This type of meat is absolutely not to be eaten by Hindus.

Ecology

Ecology

ACROSS

6   All the external conditions and factors, living and non-living, that effect an organism.
8   When small groups break off from the larger group and form a new species, the type of speciation is called ___.
10 It is a transition area between two biomes.
12 Consumers that eat both plants and animals as food.

DOWN

1   This is a type of speciation which occurs when a group is geographically separated from another group by a physical barrier.
2   This type of species is connected to a disproportionately large number of other species in the food-web.
3   These are the larger units of organization that categorize parts of the Earth's ecosystems.
4   A type of relationship between two organisms in which at least one organism benefits from the other.
5   This call of organisms is usually larger in number than heterotrophs.
7   This German scientist is often regarded as the father of ecology.
9   It is a ring-shaped reef made mostly of coral.
11 Interconnected food-___ form a food web.

Economics

Economics

ACROSS

2 A group of companies acing in unison to keep a price high and restricting competition.
6 Good produced domestically and sold abroad forms the __.
9 The ___ hand of the market supposedly brings order in free-market economics.
10 The last name of the founder of modern economics.
11 The economist who is famous for his concept of population trap.
12 It is the property of distributing economic prosperity fairly among the members of society.

DOWN

1 This is the total revenue minus the total cost.
3 The __-curve illustrates that tax beyond a level is harmful for the economy.
4 The short form for the type of GDP calculation which takes into account the price differences of common goods across nations.
5 The type of laws made against collusion, example includes the Clayton act.
7 Expansion and boom is typically followed by __ and depression in an economic cycle.
8 The law of marginal ___ often explains why gemstones are costlier than water.

Electronics

Electronics

ACROSS

2 The discover of electrons, the charge carrier in electronics.
4 A semiconductor device used to amplify or switch electrical signals. It revolutionized computing.
6 A type of device which uses continuous range of voltage or current.
7 This is a type of display technology using an organic dye in LED, with superb contrast and display color space.
8 The simplest form of battery in a circuit diagram.
10 A device which reduces the flow of a current in a circuit.
11 This is a two terminal variable resistor.
12 This is a noble gas but also a type of lamp.

DOWN

1 This device stores and releases electrical charge.
3 As opposed to series connection, bulbs should be
5 This form of diode passes current in reverse direction.
9 This device allows current to flow only in one way.

Energy(School-level)

Energy (School-level)

ACROSS

2   Th type of energy stored in batteries.
5   The type of energy which is there due to an object's rest position.
6   The particles that carry the energy in electrical wires.
7   The type of energy formed below the soil.
10 the process by which green plants harvest the energy of the sun.
11 When we exercise, we radiate energy in this form.
12 The famous scientist who found the formula E=mc^2 for stationary objects.

DOWN

1   The SI unit of energy.
3   Energy cannot be created or destroyed. this is called the law of __ of energy.
4   The energy type that was being produced in the Fukushima and Chernobyl power plants.
8   The chemical in which energy is stored in in the cells of animals.
9   The type of energy we get from the sun.

Entomology

ENTOMOLOGY

ACROSS

5 Bees do this to show the position of the food source to their hive mates.
6 A chemical substance used by insects to communicate with their own kind.
9 This insect has a social organization and is an enemy of wood.
10 The subphylum insects belong to.
11 The insect that causes the most number of deaths worldwide.
12 Bees, ants and wasps fall under this large insect order.

DOWN

1 Stomodium is the technical term of this part of the insect gut.
2 Dipteran insects have two of these and most other insects have four.
3 The Viceroy and Monarch butterfly exhibit this predator avoidance phenomena.
4 The common fruit-fly used for biological research.
7 The genus of the honeybees.
8 Coleoptera is the order of these insects.

Environmental science

Environmental Science

ACROSS
3 Liquid wastes such as sewage and liquid waste from industries.
5 Each step in a food cahin or a food web is called a __ level.
6 A large area of water surrounded by land.
10 The use of power from rising and falling ocean levels due to tides.
11 One of the prime causes of habitat loss. Results due to an excessive loss of tree cover.
12 The P in NPK fertilizers.

DOWN
1 Reversing deforestation.
2 The state of randomness in a system.
4 Waste that is thrown away like plastic bags and paper, carelessly.
7 The study of ways that organisms or living things interact with each other and with their non-living surroundings.
8 The type of rain that corrodes buildings made of marble.
9 An accumulation of organic matter produced by living things.

First Aid

First Aid

ACROSS
1   The __-cross is a famous international body for providing humanitarian assistance to the victims of war.
5   A __ (short form)should be used for people in a cardiac arrest, involving chest compression and sometimes mouth-to-mouth breathing.
8   Antivenom must be injected as soon as possible for __.
9   If a simple dressing does not stop bleeding, a __ dressing should be applied.
10 It is a condition when a particle in the airway interferes with breathing.
11 This involves breaking of a bone.
12 It occurs when there is a drastic fall in the core body temperature.

DOWN
2   Burns are divided into __ to be treated accordingly.
3   Nearest __-compression should be applied for severe bleeding that does not stop.
4   Is a life threatening shock condition due to allergies.
6   911 (In US) or 112 (In Europe) is the general __ number.
7   This bind should be used only for very severe bleeding, and removed as soon as medically possible.

Functional groups
(Chemistry)

Functional Groups(Chemistry)

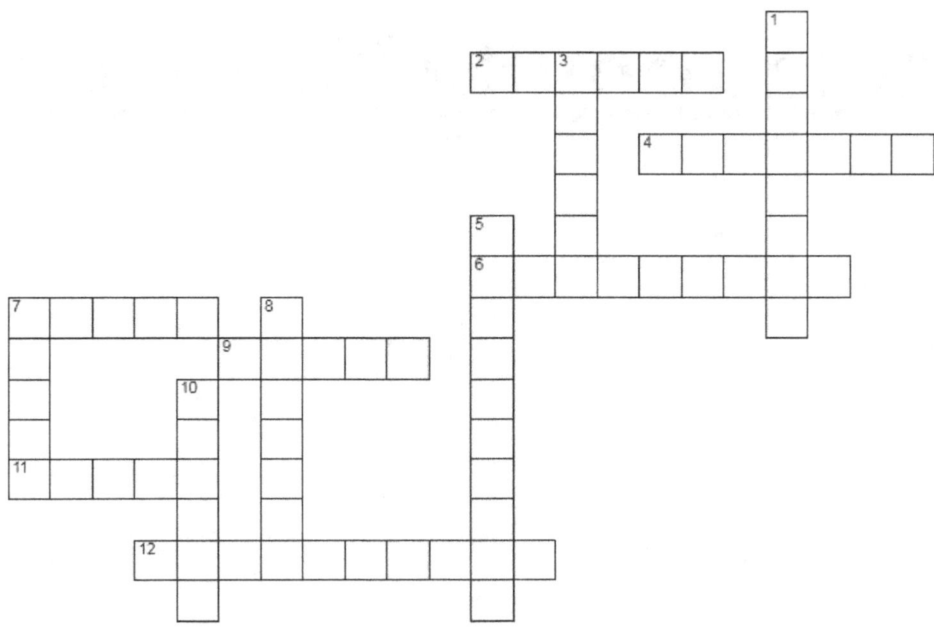

ACROSS
2   A straight chain hydrocarbon having a triple bond forms the class of:
4   These are functional groups binding to a central atom in a coordination complex.
6   This simple hydrocarbon gas is used with oxygen in welding torches.
7   Choline is a type of this chemical class.
9   The body that governs the naming of chemical compounds.
11 RN3 compounds form this general group.
12 The process by which an acid can be produced from an -ide group is called __.

DOWN
1   The type of bond which is most common in Organic Chemistry.
3   Compounds having the general formula of RCOR' is under the class of :
5   Acetic acid is a type of this acid class.
7   The first carbon after the carbon that attaches to the functional group is called the __ carbon.
8   Thiol groups have this unique element.
10 The circular group in Benzene is termed as __ group.

Geography(School-Level)

Geography(School-Level)

ACROSS

2 The imaginary circle dividing the Earth horizontally.
6 The continent which has the largest hot desert.
7 A compact body of land entirely surrounded by water.
8 A narrow neck of land joining two larger bodies of land.
9 A small hill.
11 The largest island.
12 The longest river in Europe.

DOWN

1 This is a device which is used to find the direction when in field.
3 The popular scale for measuring the strength of earthquakes.
4 The ___-trench is the deepest point of the ocean.
5 The deepest freshwater lake (found in Russia).
10 A diagram of a geographical region drawn to scale. Usually in the form of physical
   features, township or altitude.

Geological Time Scale

Geological Time Scale

ACROSS
4   The period preceding the greatest mass-extinction.
5   Eons are divided into ___s.
6   A living fossil plant(genus name) which is said to survive the nuclear blast in Hiroshima.
7   The Chicxulub impact, near present day ___(country) caused the K-T extinction.
9   The class for armored fishes which dominated in the Devonian.
10 The larger continents like Pangaea which divided to make the continents of today.
11 Large scale movement of plates to change the structure of the continents is termed as plate-___.
12 The ___-dating process is often used to determine the age of rocks.

DOWN
1   Permian and Devonian periods fall under this era.
2   The Great-___ event was probably the first mass extinction.
3   Very early in the history of the Earth, a collision broke a part of the planet and formed the ___.
8   The period when most of the major phyla originated.

Geometry

Geometry

ACROSS

2 A surface(type of strip) which has only one side, often shown in a party trick involving paper.

4 A type of 4-sided non-rectangular polygon whose area is generally calculated by the formula base*height.

6 Portion of a disk enclosed by two radii and an arc.

8 Mathematician whose theorem is used to calculate the area of any triangle (scalene).

9 This type of plane and geometry is required for the sum of the interior angles of a triangle to be 180 degrees.

10 When an angle is less than 90 degrees, it is called ___.

11 An instrument to draw perfect circles.

DOWN

1 When two triangles have their corresponding angles congruent and proportional corresponding sides, they are called ___.

3 An instrument used to measure geometrical angles.

5 The basic one dimensional object of geometry.

6 A three dimensional analog of the circle.

7 A part of the circumference of a circle.

Human Body

Human Body

ACROSS
7 The type of joint in the knee and elbow.
8 A functional unit of the kidney.
9 The technical term of nearsightedness, which requires wearing glasses.
10 This gland is called the master gland as it controls many other glands of the body.
11 The short-form of the cells in the blood that carries oxygen.

DOWN
1 The pipe that connects the mouth to the stomach.
2 The innermost part of bone that produces blood cells.
3 The biggest organ in human body.
4 The substance that make up our nails.
5 The longest bone in the human body.
6 The tiniest bone in the human body.
7 The DNA has a double ___ structure.

Internet

Internet

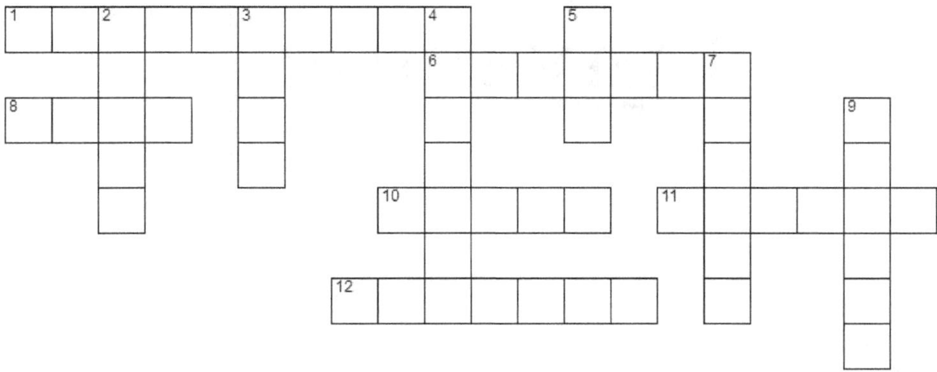

ACROSS
1   It is the scrambling of data to prevent eavesdroppers in a connection.
6   The most popular mobile OS on which the internet is accessed from.
8   An online journal for public view.
10 A secure form of HTTP which is almost universal these days.
11 The common browser used to access the internet from apple devices.
12 The very popular internet browser by Mozilla.

DOWN
2   Online storage is often called by this name.
3   A type of internet query done to see if the computer is connected to the internet or not.
4   The first wide scale music sharing service.
5   The domain extension for organizations.
7   The address of a website is also called its __.
9   The computers that serve the contents of the internet.

Inventors

Inventors

ACROSS

6 He is the inventor of the popular programming language C.
8 Tim-Berners Lee is credited as the inventor of this spectacular modern invention.
9 The inventor of the steam engine.
10 Called the inventor of the light bulb, had more than 1000 inventions.
11 The inventor of the modern moving assembly line, which brought a huge change in modern manufacturing.

DOWN

1 Considered to be the father of computers.
2 A brilliant British physicist, the SI unit of force is named after him.
3 The discoverer of the first antibiotic, penicillin.
4 Best known mathematician and scientist of ancient times, invented a screw used for irrigation.
5 The inventor of alternating current.
6 The discoverer of X-rays.
7 Discovered the pasteurization process of milk preservation.

Laboratory Science

Laboratory science

ACROSS

5 A common laboratory method of quantitative chemical analysis used to determine the concentration of an identified analyte.
6 A study based on lab diagnosis of bodily fluids and tissues.
8 A device used to increase moisture in an environment.
11 A type of scale used to measure distances more precisely than ordinary scales.
12 A pressure chamber with high temperature used to sterilize biological equipment.

DOWN

1 A lab instrument used to cut extremely thin sections of tissues by a thin blade.
2 The H in pH stands for ___.
3 An instrument using a motor which is used to spin liquids to separate layers.
4 Biological substance that poses a hazard to humans or other animals.
7 A liquid solution containing a combination of chemicals, which control and maintain the pH of a solution it is added to.
9 A type of open gas flame burner using a valve, which is very common in chemistry laboratories.
10 These are used in the lab to prevent the injury or contamination of hands.

Logic and Sets

Logic and Sets

ACROSS

3 This set of a set A is the set whose members are all of the possible subsets of A.
7 Addition is performed by logic gates which are connected together, forming this object.
9 A type of logic gate which means not-AND.
10 This set is the set of all objects that are members of both the two sets in question.
11 Often regarded as the father of set-theory.

DOWN

1 A type of very popular algebra pioneered by George Boole.
2 The name given to the type of diagram which we commonly use to simplify set diagrams, composed of circles.
4 If a set is contained in another set, it is called by this name.
5 the set that contains all the elements.
6 The set that contains elements or objects that belong to two sets separately, or in both of them.
7 A type of logic gate which will output 1 if both the inputs are 1.
8 A type of logic gate which will output 1 only if just one of its inputs is 1.

<u>Metals(School-Level)</u>

Metals (School-level)

ACROSS

3 This silvery metal is the one from which the metal got the adjective.
4 This metal is used to make wires in electricity lines.
5 This metal is good for our bones and teeth.
8 Stainless steel usually have this metal at-least in a proportion greater than 10 percent.
9 This radioactive metal can be utilized to make atomic bombs. It is also used as a type of mineral dating.
10 This metal is used to make jewellery which is even more expensive than gold.
11 Rust is known to form in this metal.

DOWN

1 This yellow metal is very precious.
2 This is the only liquid metal.
3 This is a metallic element found in table salt.
6 This whitish metal is used to make utensils and is also used to wrap food by a foil.
7 The metal found in bulb filaments, has a very high melting point.

Mobile Phones

Mobile phones

ACROSS
6   A new type of fingerprint scanner that can be placed under the display.
7   A type of mobile display where the blacks are represented by near-total darkness and the lack of backlighting.
9   The three letters that represent the battery capacity in short.
10 A Taiwanese brand of mobile phones, once used to manufacture Windows mobiles too.
11 A mandatory hardware instrument in mobile phones that is mandatory to be able to take Photo-Spheres in camera applications.

DOWN
1   Was the largest mobile phone company, now the brand-name is used by HMD.
2   The google line of phones, which are priced at the premium range.
3   The G is 4G stands for this.
4   The rare type of glass used in some apple phones which is much stronger than gorilla glass and can also be a gemstone.
5   A trend that ran after the introduction of iPhone 8, where the top part of the display is not symmetrical to the bottom.

8   The most widely used phone operating system in the world.

Nursing

Nursing

ACROSS

2 Swelling caused by excess fluid in the body tissues.
6 This process involves using a needle to push a drug through the skin.
7 The side opposite to ventral.
8 A __ is a piece of cloth is applied to bind up an wound.
10 It is a type of lotion/solution used to prevent the growth of disease-causing microorganisms.
12 Florence __ was a prominent figure in the development of modern nursing.

DOWN

1 Syncope is commonly known as __.
3 The technical term for fever.
4 This is the technical term for spitting up blood.
5 It the process of eating the right balance of foods for healthy living.
9 In case of an emergency, ___, breathing and circulation(ABC)should be paid well attention to.
11 A __ shock is a result of infection,causing organ failure and very low blood pressure.

Particle Physics

Particle Physics

ACROSS
3 Photons of the highest wavelength are classified as _-waves.
6 Neutral leptons are called __.
8 Objects have an wave-___ duality.
10 This type of matter does not interact electromagnetically but is supposed to quantify for a lot of mass in the universe.
11 Electrons are usually in this state in their orbitals, but they can also be in the excited state.
12 This scientist is known as the father of quantum mechanics.

DOWN
1 The standard model has 24 types of this particle.
2 Protons and neutrons are composite particles called ___.
4 The standard model has __ species of elementary particles.
5 Baryons are made up of __.
7 the first lepton to be discovered.
9 Photons of the lowest wavelength are classified as _-rays.

Periodic Table

Periodic Table

ACROSS

2   SI unit of the amount of substance contained in 12 grams of carbon 12.
5   The periodic symbol of mercury.
6   The Latin name of the element used in the filament of light bulbs.
8   The most electronegative of all the elements.
10 The lightest element whose isotopes are all radioactive.

DOWN

1   The group of metals which are monovalent and produce strong alkaline hydroxides.
3   The non-metal that is liquid in room temperature(>30 degrees)
4   The Latin name of iron from which the symbol Fe originates.
5   The most abundant noble gas in the universe.
7   The element named after the scientist who discovered radioactivity.
9   Most radioactive elements decay to this element.
11 The metal used in electric wires, having a reddish-brown color.

Physics

Physics

ACROSS

6 The planet whose fine measurement of orbit supported Einstein's theory.
8 Whose law about pressure makes hydraulic brakes work.
11 The physicist after whom the famous cat thought experiment is named.
12 The name of the force which binds neutrons and protons together in the nucleus.

DOWN

1 A branch of physics dealing with light.
2 The scale our body temperature is usually measured in.
3 A simple machine which reduces the friction of moving objects.
4 The unit of force.
5 The famous physicist who predicted that black holes are not truly black.
7 A packet of light is called by this name.
9 The proposed one-dimensional fundamental particle.
10 The Indian physicist after whom a group of fundamental particles is named.

Planet Earth

Planet Earth

ACROSS
7   The other name of Earth's moon.
9   The third most common gas in Earth's atmosphere.
10 The lowermost layer of the atmosphere.
12 The deepest lake of the world.

DOWN
1   Sand is made up of this element and oxygen.
2   The moment when the Equator passes through the center of the sun's disk.
3   When magma comes out of the surface, it is called __ .
4   The rocky parts of the Earth's crust is known as-
5   The super-continent from which the modern continents originated.
6   The most abundant element in Earth's crust.
8   The layer of Earth below the crust.
11 The largest ocean.

Programming

Programming

ACROSS

2 This is a process done to catch bugs in a software code.
4 Variables which stores words are usually stored in this data type.
5 These are sentences in written language in the code, usually to make it more easy to understand.
7 A multimedia technology for websites which has gained obsolescence due to its security flaws.
8 These values are either true or false.
10 A structure which contains elements assigned by a single index. the common form is one-dimensional.
11 Linus Torvalds, a famous programmer, is known for the development of the kernel of this OS.
12 8 bits make one __.

DOWN

1 Visual Basic, the popular programming language, is developed by __.
3 A very low level language often used to write kernels.
6 THE # in C# is pronounced as __.
9 The company that owns Java.

Psychology

Psychology.

ACROSS

4 The organ that regulates thinking.
5 The scientist who is widely known for his experiment with conditioning in dogs.
6 The doubted means of transfer of information on thoughts or feelings from one mind to another without the use sensory perceptions.
8 It is an involuntary and fast movement in response to a stimulus.
11 The scientist who is famous for his inkblot test in psychology.
12 Maslow's hierarchy refers ti the pyramid of ___.

DOWN

1 The IQ test stands for Intelligence ___.
2 the type of psychology which stresses on how lineages evolved over time.
3 A popular test which divides people upon 16 personalities.
7 In psychology, it is described as excessive psychological dependence on a particular thing.
9 This includes informed and voluntary consent for experiments. The Stanford-prison experiment violated this.
10 The Austrian scientist who is regarded as the founder of psychoanalysis.

SI units

SI Units

ACROSS

2 Unit of magnetic flux.
6 Farad is the unit of this quantity.
7 Unit of inductance.
9 Unit of mass.
10 The unit of current.
11 This quantity is measured in Hertz.
12 Unit of absorbed dose of radiation.

DOWN

1 Prefix denoting 10^21
3 The unit of solid angle.
4 The unit of radioactivity.
5 SI is the modern form of the __ system.
8 The unit of luminous intensity.

Stars

Stars

ACROSS

5 The closest star to our planet.
8 When light stars burst open into (often)beautiful diffused clouds.
9 The R is H-R diagram in the context of stars stands for:
10 The brightest star in the night sky.
11 We measure the brightness of star by this term. It can be apparent or absolute.
12 The type of star has the highest density and is made up of primarily one of the nucleons.

DOWN

1 The layer responsible for the twinkling of the stars.
2 The full one word name of the Pole star.
3 Super and Red are used as prefixes to this type of star.
4 The basic fuel of stars.
6 This is not a star at all but is called the morning star.
7 The process that causes the stars to emit light.

Statistics

Statistics

ACROSS

2 Collecting the opinions of a group of people by asking them questions.
3 Very popular open-source statistical calculation software.
6 This statistical term is the square of standard deviation.
8 The shorthand for Analysis of Variance.
12 A statistical data should be this to be considered important.

DOWN

1 The more common term for 'mean'.
4 The term for the collection of data.
5 The founder of mathematical statistics.
7 The middle term in a sorted list of data.
9 A type of hypothesis denoting default position that there is no relation between two variables.
10 The Greek symbol for simple summation.
11 A a rectangular array of numbers for which addition and multiplication are defined.

Theory of Relativity

Theory of Relativity

ACROSS

1. The Annus-___ are the three seminal papers of Einstein in 1905. These laid to much of the foundations of modern physics.
6. Einstein was born in this country.
8. The speed of ___ being constant in vacuum is one of the postulates of special relativity.
9. Moving clocks tick at a slower rate through the eyes of a distant observer. This is called time-___.
11. The length of an object in a moving frame appears shortened to an observer, the amount is calculated by ___-contraction.
12. Rotating objects drag space-time around them. this is known as ___-dragging.

DOWN

2. Distant objects in the universe show gravitational ___(ing), illustrating the lengthening of wavelengths.
3. Invariance and unification of physical quantities both arise from four-___.
4. ___'s equations for electromagnetism is strongly linked with Einstein's theory.
5. Special relativity superseded this form of relativity, named after a famous Italian astronomer.
7. Gravitational ___ can show the rear of a massive object such as a black hole due to the large distortion of space-time.
10. The Einstein fields equations involve metric-___.

Windows

Windows

ACROSS
4   A place to store bits of information for programs in Windows.
5   The program deleted in windows 10 builds which is replaced by a modern 3D alternative.
6   The default hardware which the first letter of the alphabet represented in drives.
7   The short command that runs the Command Prompt.
10 Name of the very popular default wallpaper of windows XP.
11 The wallpaper analog which was deprecated due to CRTs getting out of fashion.
12 Windows often boot into this.

DOWN
1   A special folder that supports a simple two-way file synchronization between itself and another folder in Windows.
2   The command in "run" to configure boot and general services.
3   The codename of Windows Vista before it was formally announced.
8   The anti-virus that comes preinstalled with windows.
9   The colored screen of death, after a fatal system error.

Zoology

Zoology

ACROSS
1. Animals which are specialized to live in trees.
5. The coiling of the body in molluscs is also known as __.
6. This is the study of animal behavior.
7. the yellow part of an egg.
8. This ancient philosopher is known as the father of Zoology.
9. The long pointed tooth, longer in carnivores, which is used to tear flesh.
10. An animal which eats fruits as their main source of nutrients.
11. A type of species which is restricted to a specific geographic region.

DOWN
2. A subclass of reptiles which has no temporal openings in the skull.
3. Evolution study is mostly the study of fossils, otherwise known as __.
4. A single specimen used as a type to name and describe a set of species and subspecies.
9. A tortoise's shell is also called its __.

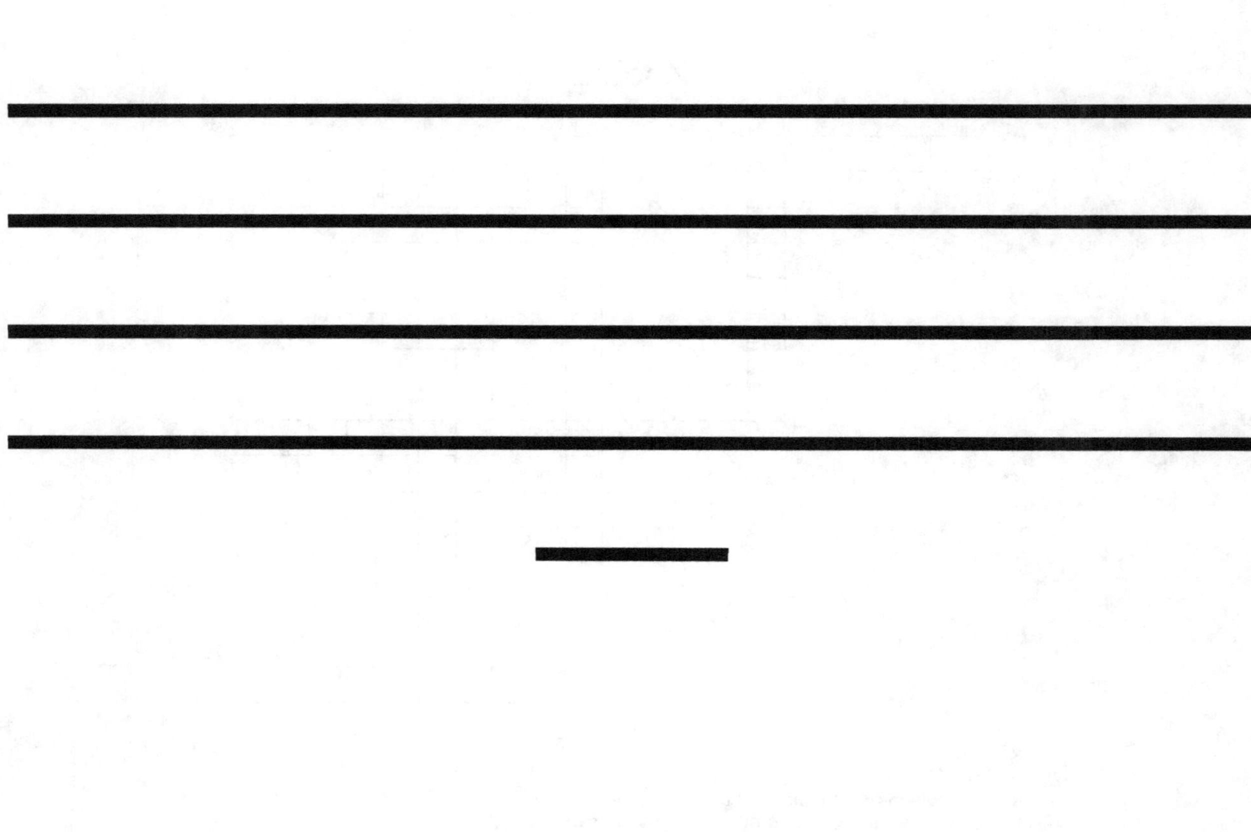

ANSWERS

Zoology

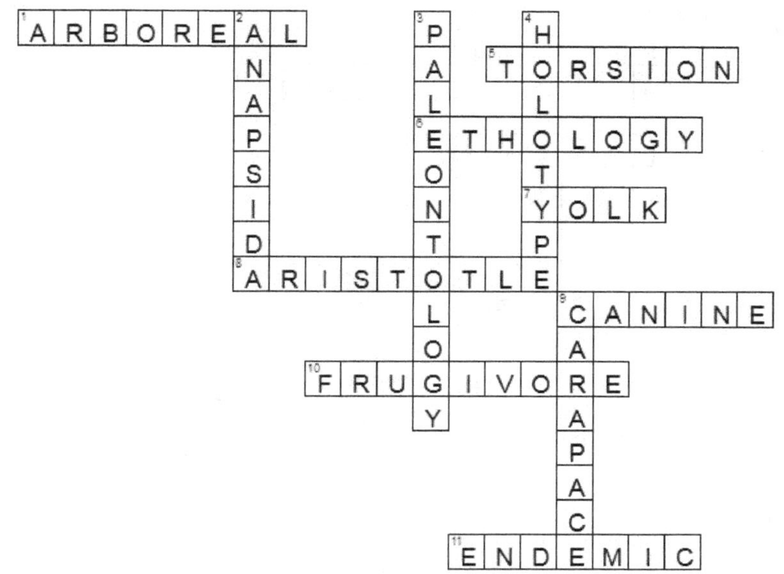

Theory of Relativity

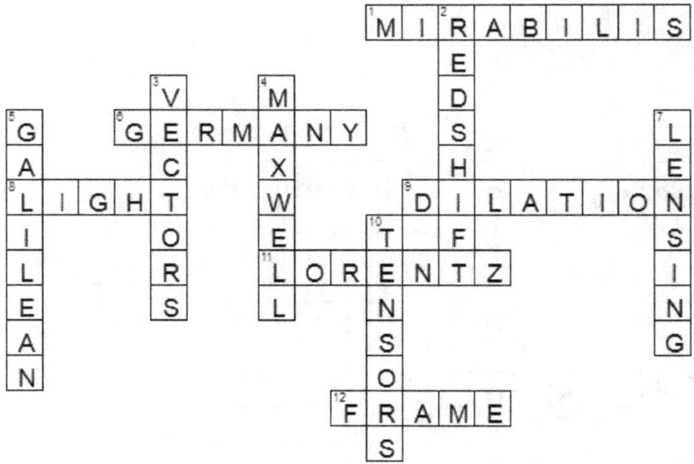

Statistics

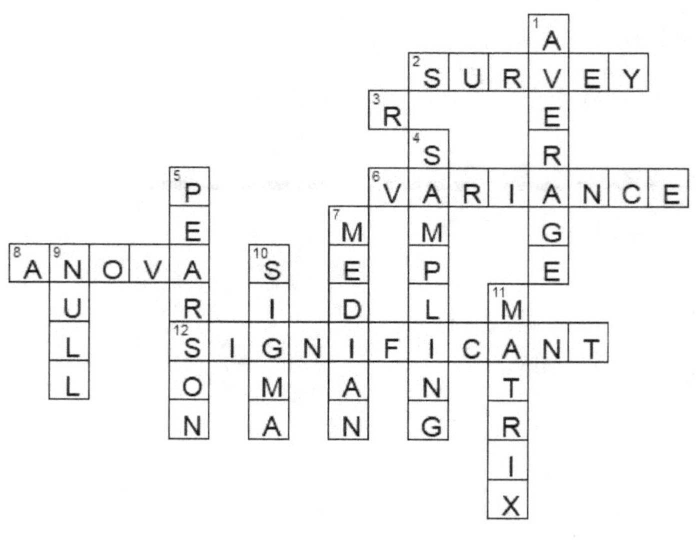

Stars

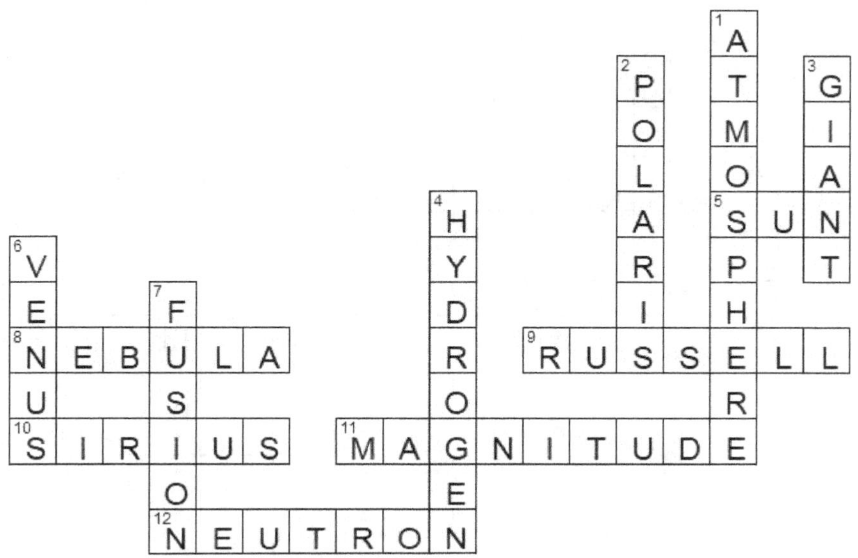

SI Units

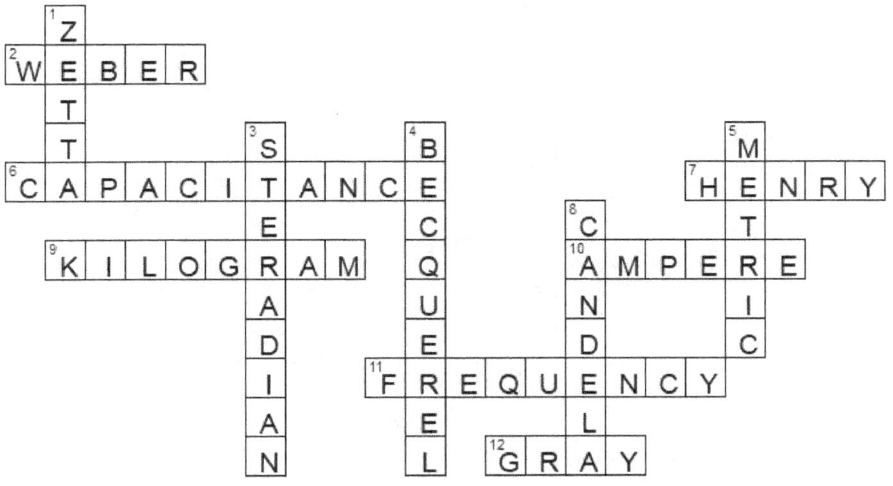

Psychology.

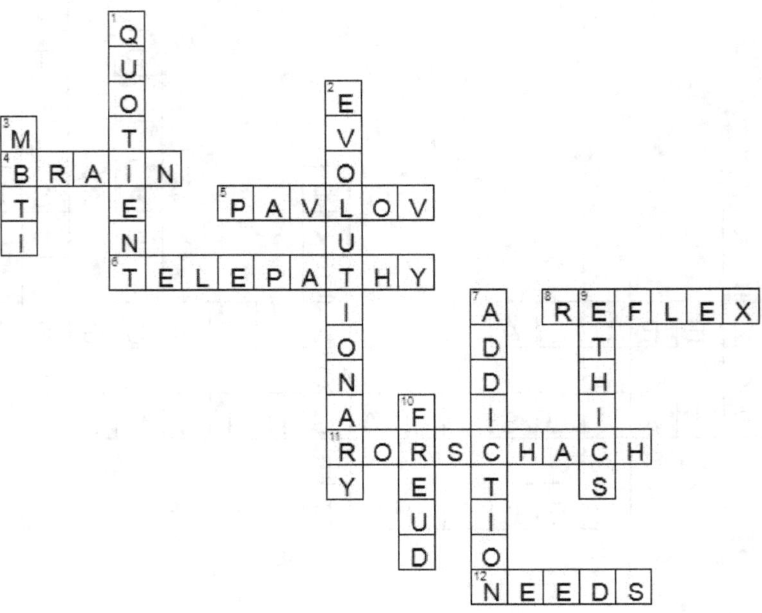

Programming

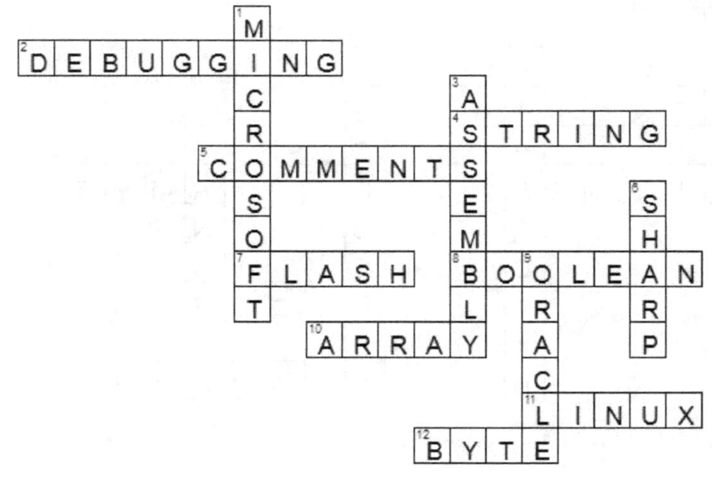

Planet Earth

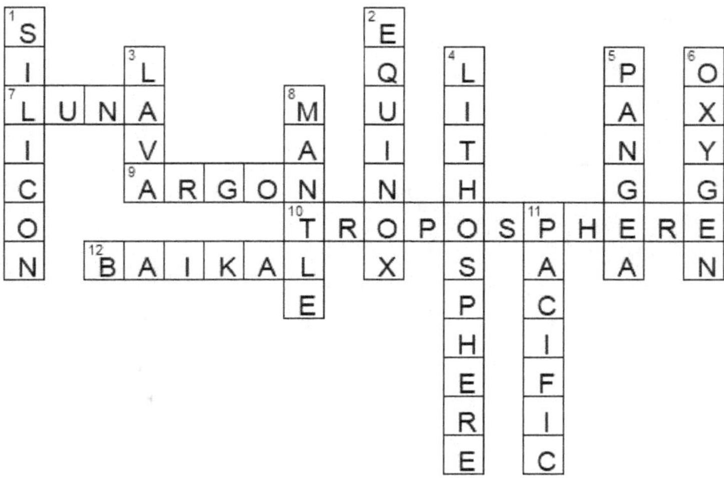

Physics

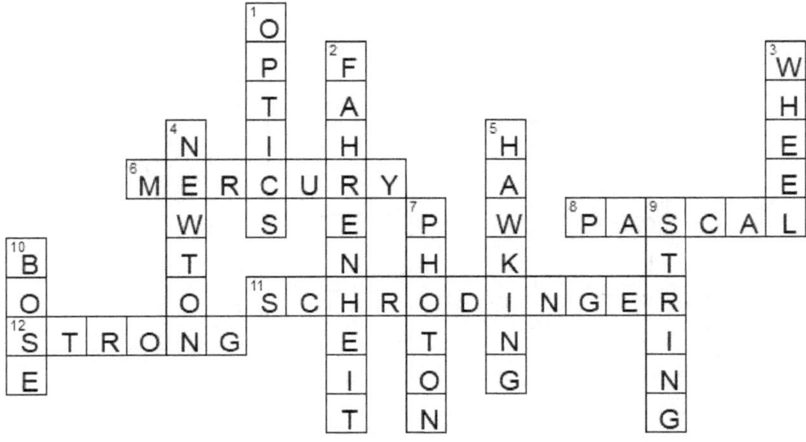

Periodic Table

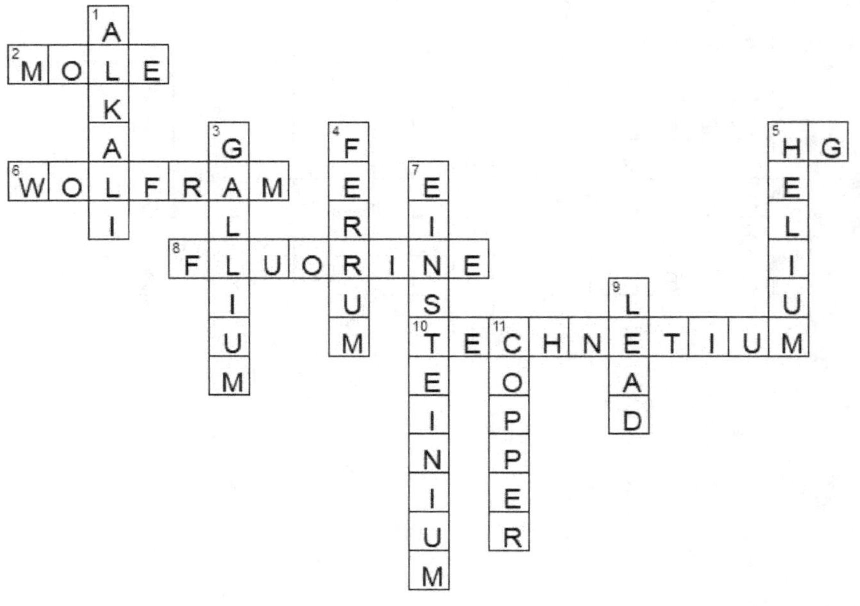

Particle Physics

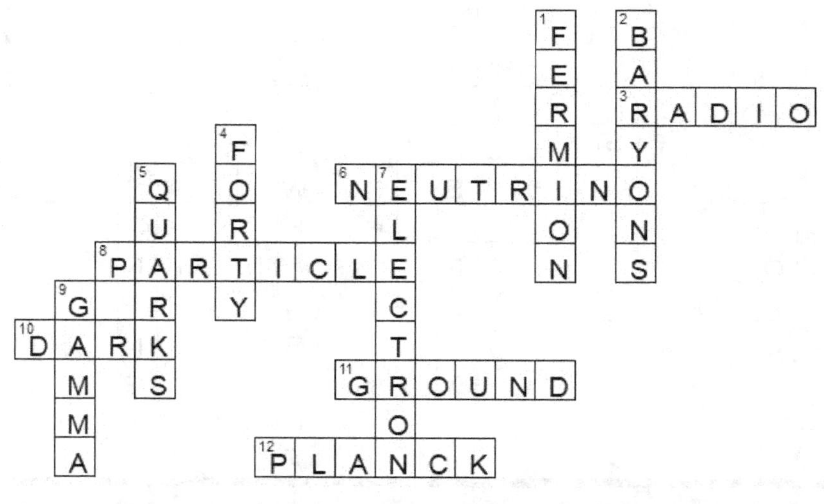

Nursing

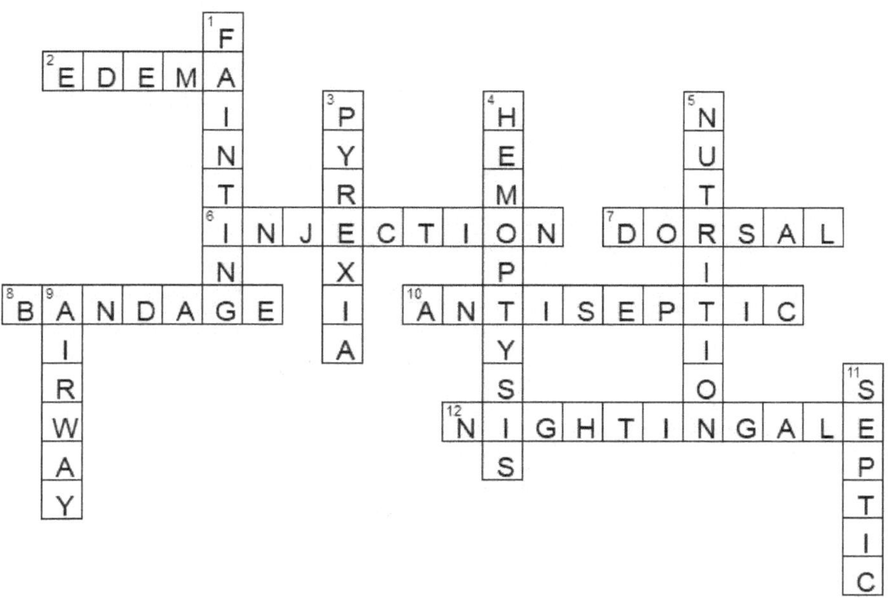

Metals (School-level)

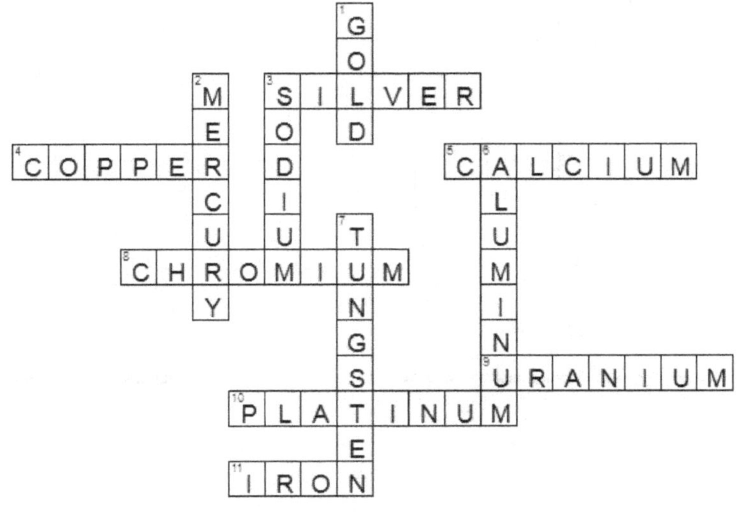

Logic and Sets

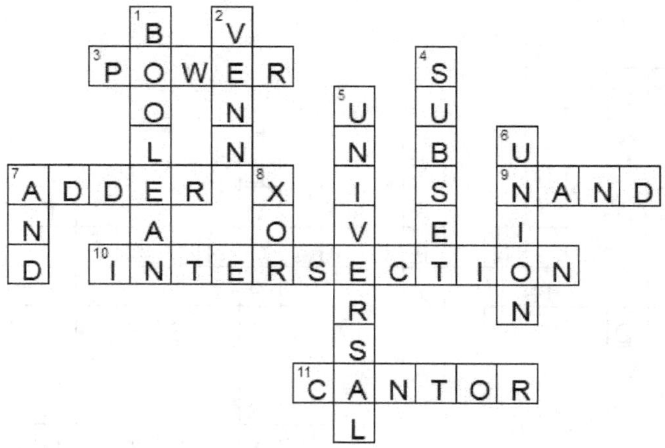

Laboratory science

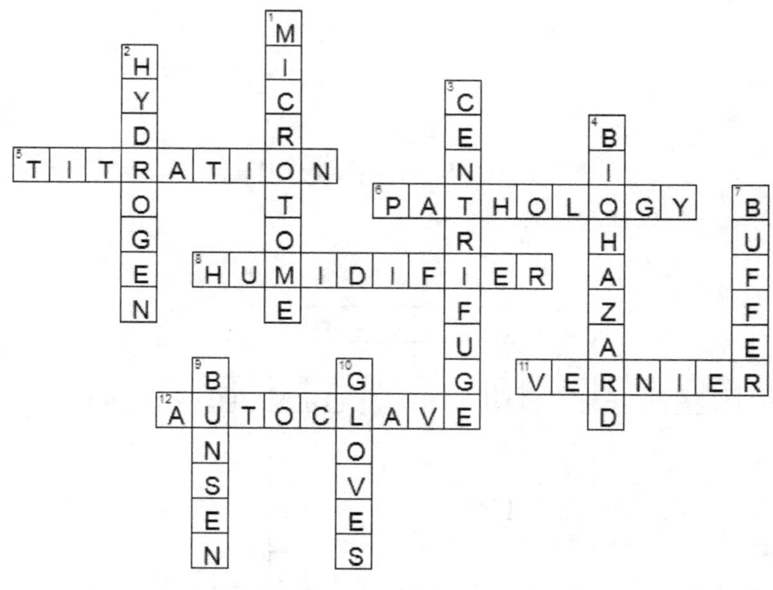

Inventors

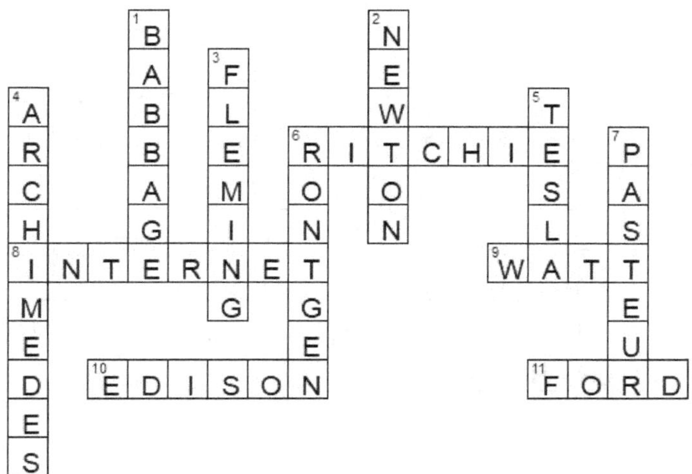

Internet

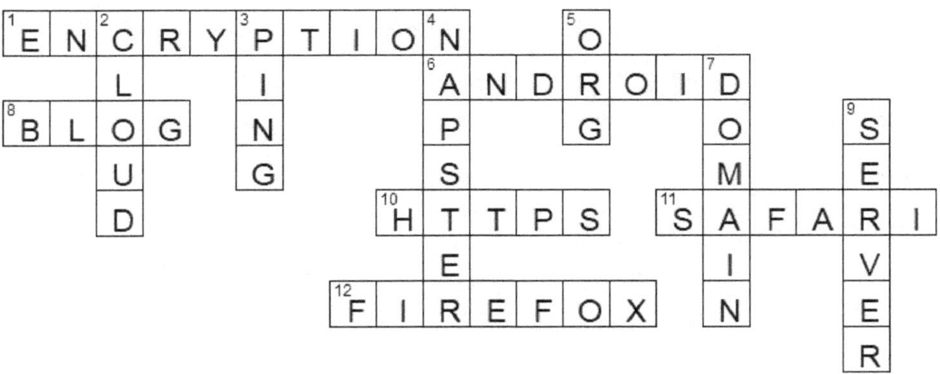

Human Body

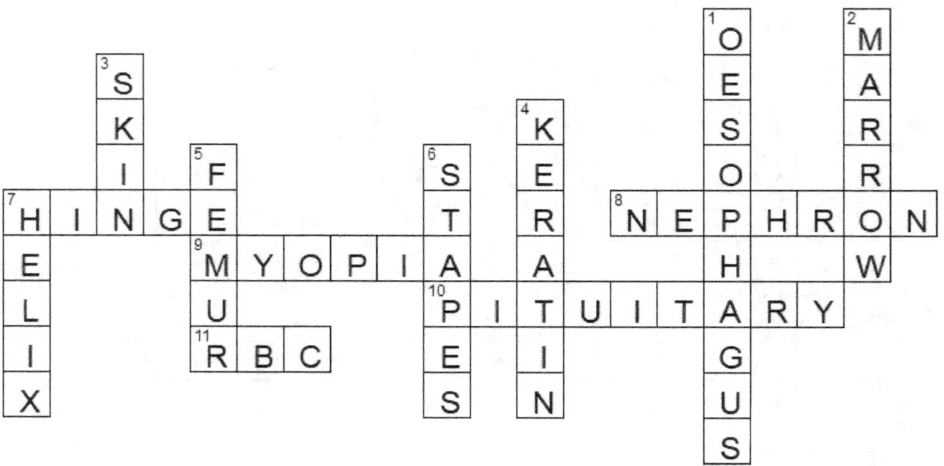

Geometry

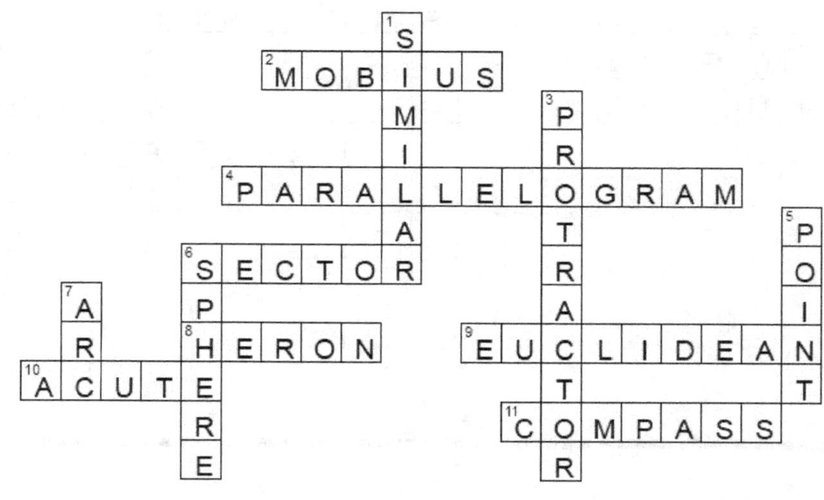

Geological Time Scale

Geography(School-Level)

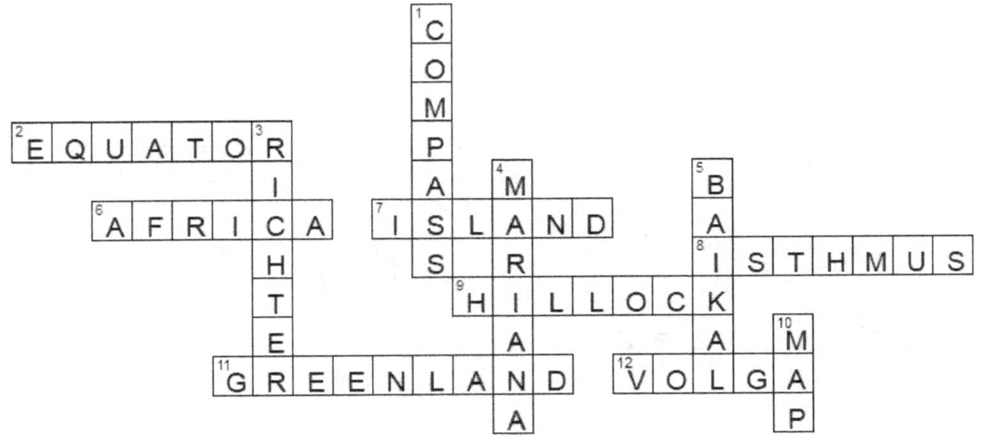

Functional Groups(Chemistry)

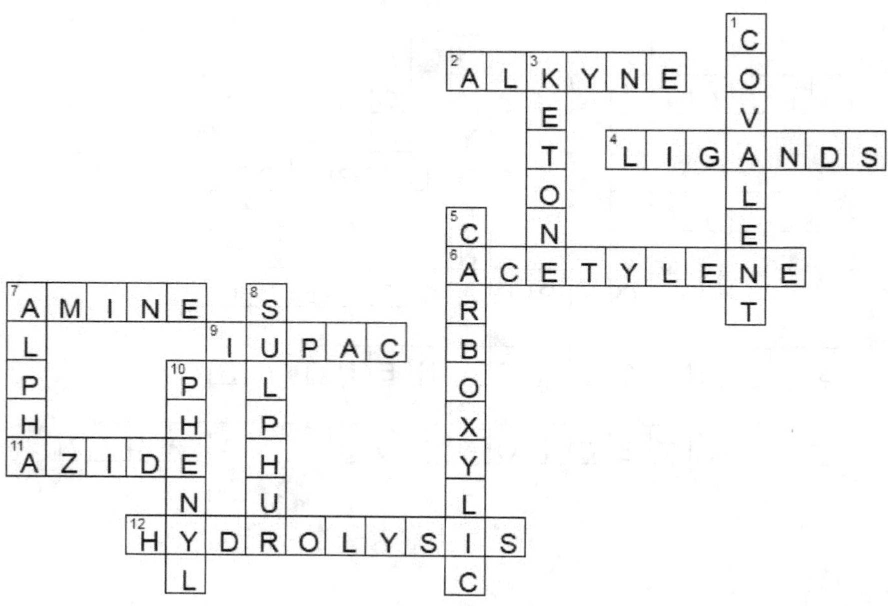

First Aid

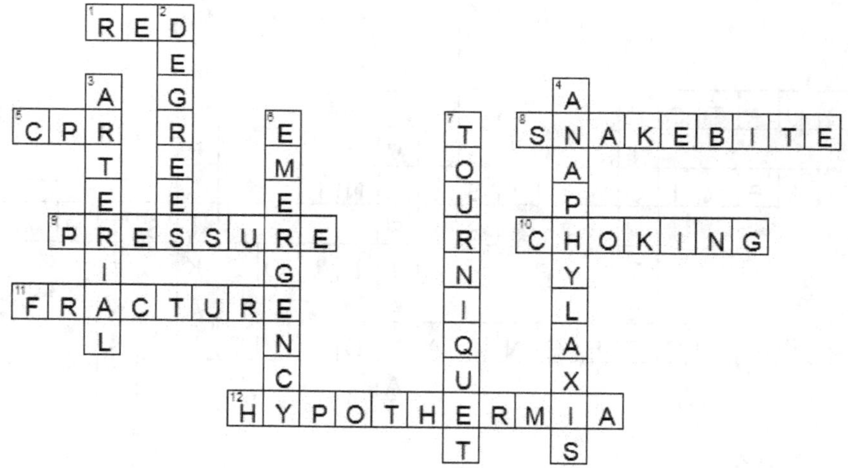

Environmental Science

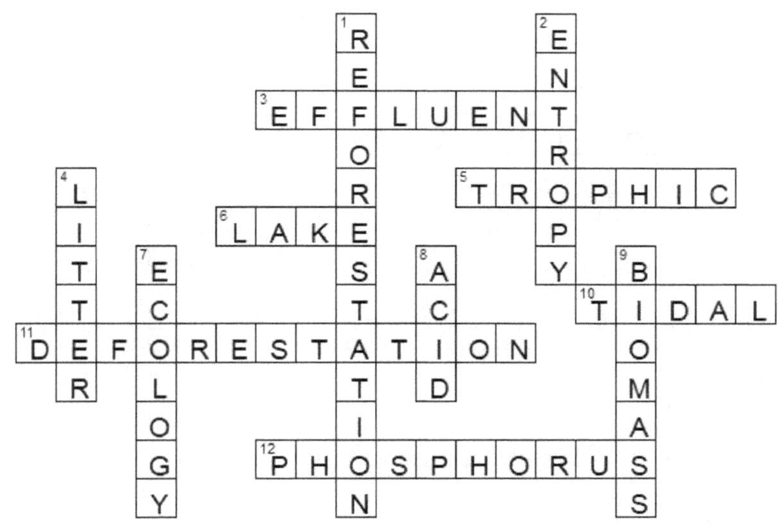

ENTOMOLOGY

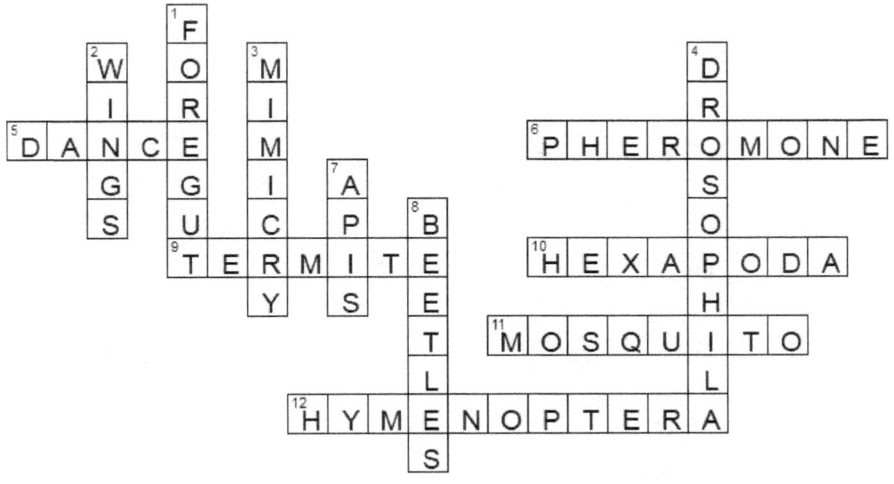

Energy (School-level)

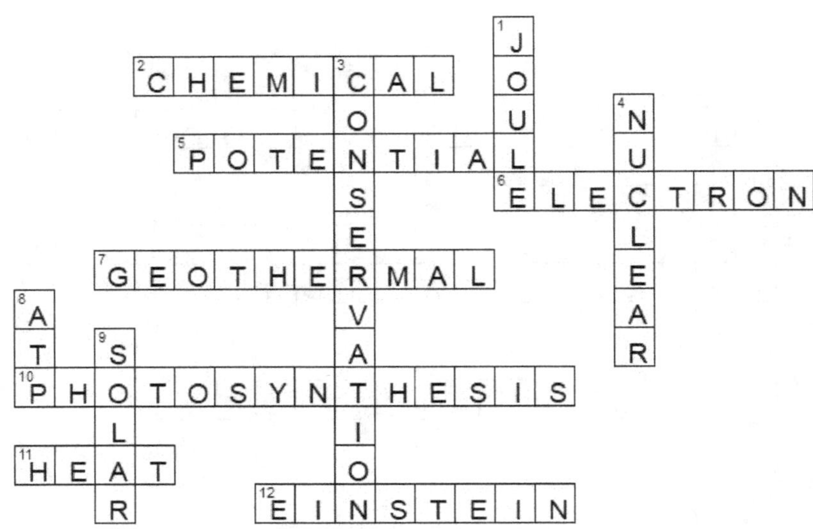

Electronics

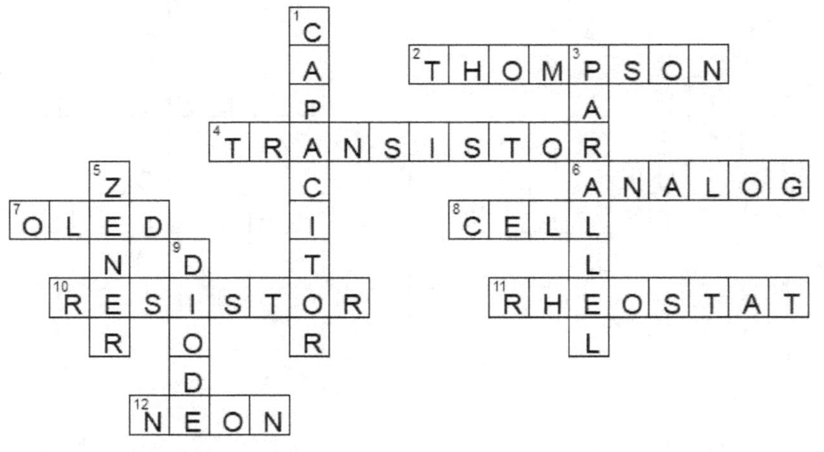

Economics

Ecology

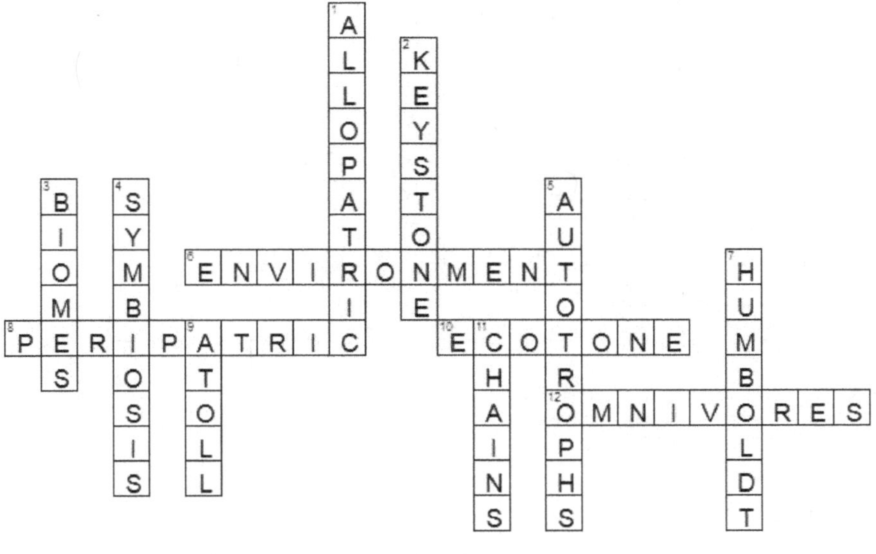

Diet

Computer hardware(School Level)

Cognitive Science

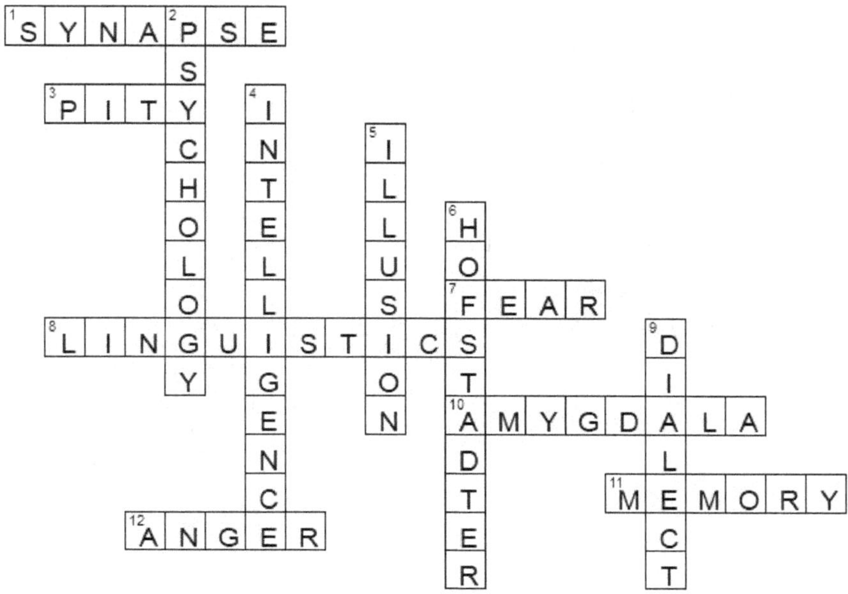

Clouds

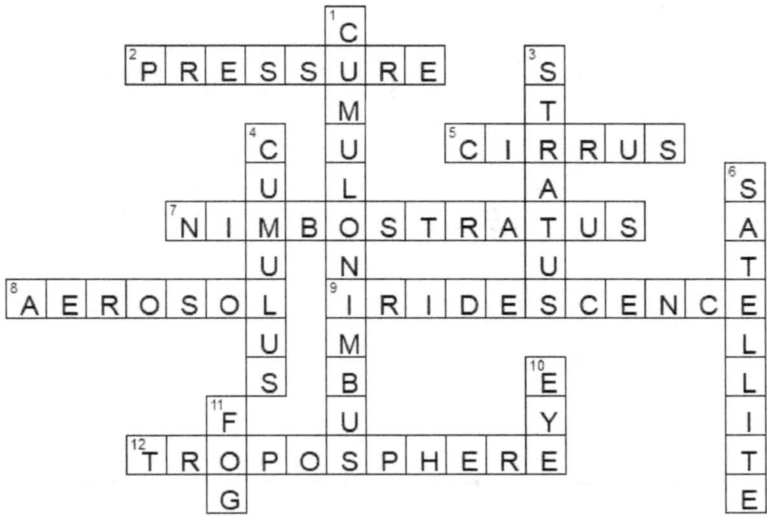

Chemistry

Cell(Biology)

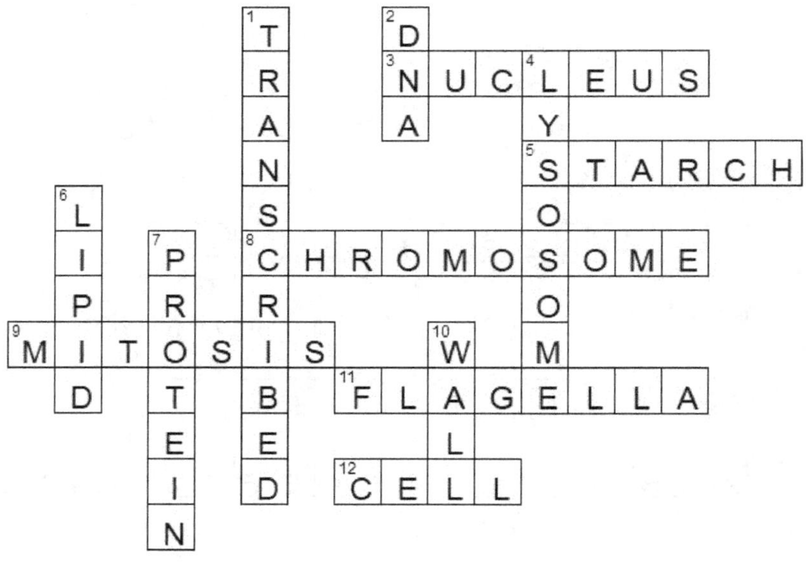

Biology

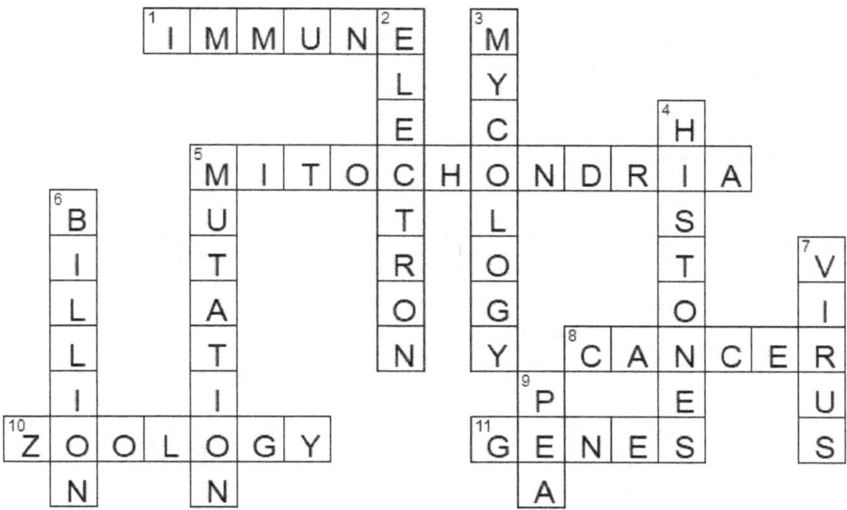

Biogeochemical Cycle (School-Level)

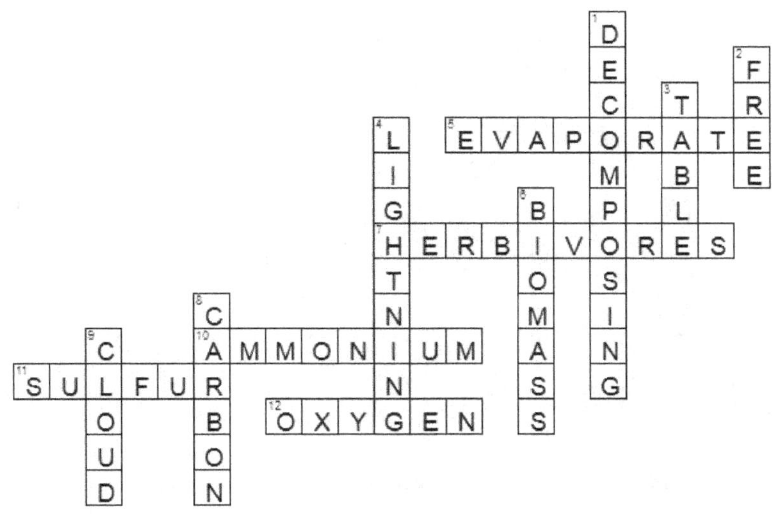

Astronomy

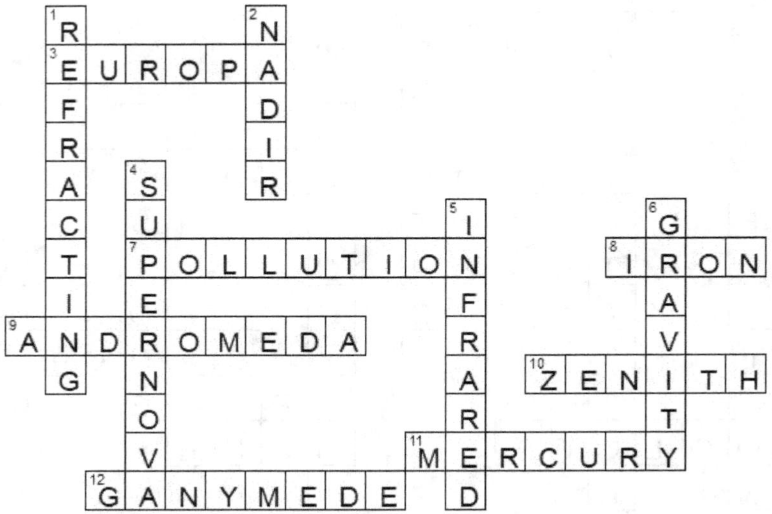

Animals

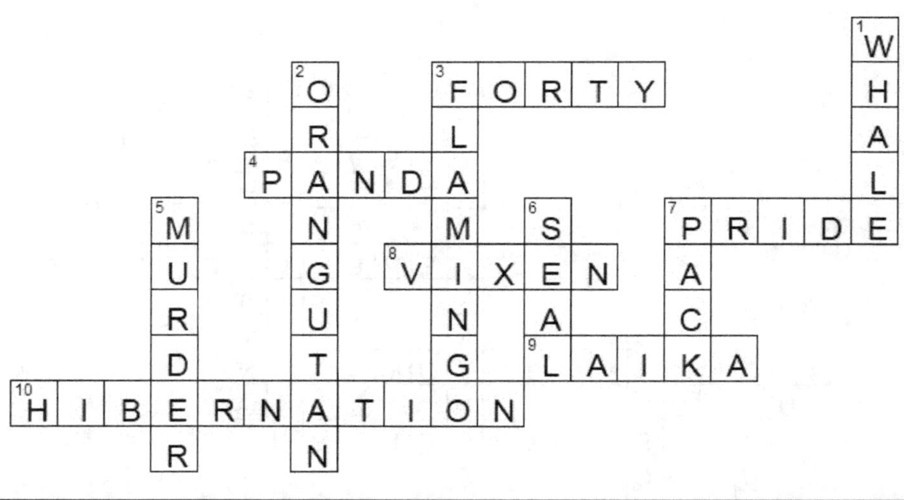

Animal Classification(Nonchordates)

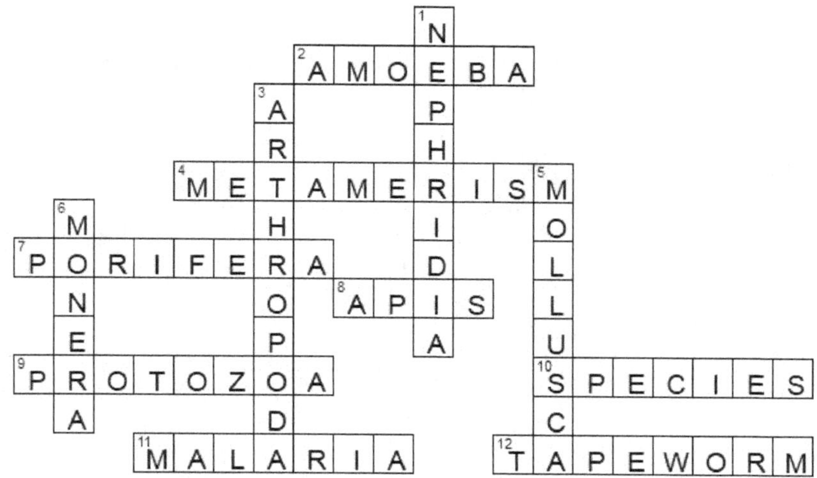

Animal Classification(Chordates)

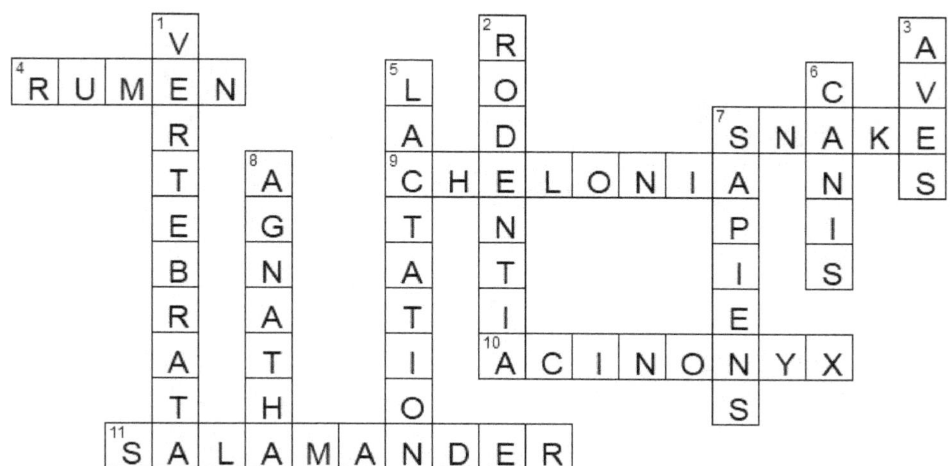

Agricultural science

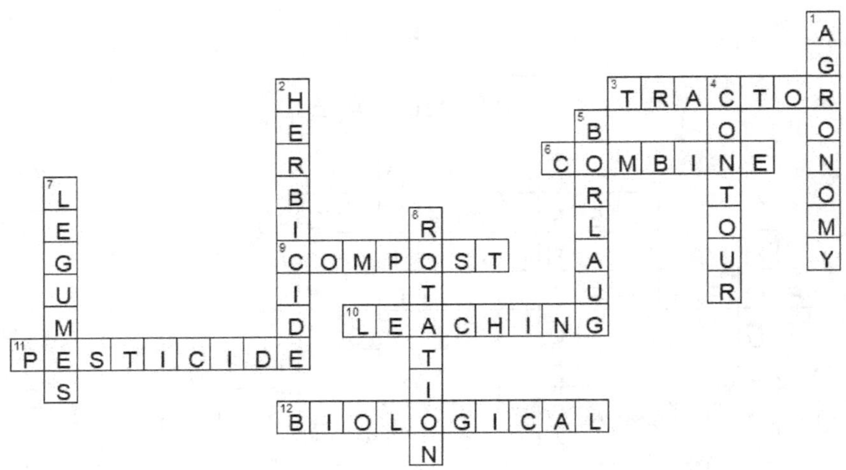

www.ingramcontent.com/pod-product-compliance
Lightning Source LLC
Chambersburg PA
CBHW081437250726
48662CB00009B/2831